MW00653422

Taking a break on Azure Mountain.

D🐾G HIKES
IN THE
ADIRONDACKS

20 Trails to Enjoy with Your Best Friend

EDITED BY

Annie Stoltie &

Elisabeth Ward

ALL PHOTOGRAPHS BY

Nancie Battaglia

Unless Otherwise Noted

SHAGGY DOG PRESS

WESTPORT, NY 2009

Published by
SHAGGY DOG PRESS

PO Box 318
Westport, NY 12993

shaggydogpress@aol.com
www.shaggydogpress.org

Design: **SUSAN BIBEAU**

Cover & back-cover photographs: **NANCIE BATTAGLIA**

Printing: **QUEEN CITY PRINTERS, INC.** Burlington, VT

ISBN: 978-0-9722007-3-8

**Proceeds from the sale of this guide
benefit the animal shelters and humane
organizations in the Adirondack Park.**

When buying or ordering this book online
(**www.shaggydogpress.org**)
please state a preferred recipient.

Otherwise all proceeds automatically go to the
North Country Society for the Prevention
of Cruelty to Animals (NCSPCA) in Westport.

CONTENTS

A Cascade Mountain summit meeting.

Hiking with Dogs in the Adirondack Park

The Adirondack Park, six million acres of forested hills, rolling pastures, rock-encrusted peaks and glittering lakes, sits south of Quebec, east of the St. Lawrence River, west of Lake Champlain and north of Albany. Elevation climbs from Lake Champlain, at 90 feet above sea level, to Mount Marcy at 5,343 feet.

This paradise for outdoor activities envelops a mix of towns and state-owned and private lands. The population explodes in the summer, grows slightly with winter sports enthusiasts around Christmas and the Presidents Day holiday, and is truly reflected during the shoulder seasons by hunters and maple-syrup makers. The major rivers—Hudson, Schroon, Raquette, Saranac, Ausable and Essex County's own Boquet—are fished and canoed whenever they're not iced in.

Thousands of hiking trails lead through mixed hardwoods and conifers of all sorts; along lakes, over bridges and across boardwalks that protect fragile bogs or swamp muck, to the mightiest tops of the High Peaks and into the tenderest of valleys.

Most of these trails are open to the public. Most allow dogs, even horses. In both cases the animals must be under control of a human. Leash laws are always in effect for the High Peaks. Many trails lead to campsites—and many do not. Be sure to know the rules that apply to yours. Most have registration boxes at the trailhead. Signing in before starting a hike is the smart thing to do.

We've chosen 20 hikes of varying stages of difficulty for this, our introductory, guide. We owe a large thank you to all those writers who gathered their dogs, water bottles and dog treats to jot down their experiences on the trail. Thanks also to Al Haberle, DVM, of Westport.

Thank you to *Adirondack Life* magazine for permission to use the articles by Elizabeth Folwell (Introducing the Young Pup to the Trail, Sawyer, Goodnow, Crane Pond hikes, and State Campground information), Mary Thill (Dewey hike and Additional Facts), Annie Stoltie (First Brother) and Joanne Kennedy (Poke-O-Moonshine).

Thank you to Sue Bibeau, of Saranac Lake, for offering her excellent design skills.

And a giant—or even a mountainous—thank you to Nancie Battaglia, of Lake Placid, for her incredible photographs for the canine cause.

Truly, dog lovers are the best!

The Adirondack Park remains uncrowded by the grace of location. The closest large city is Montreal. New York and Boston are five-hour drives away. The pet population may well challenge that of humans, which helps to explain the number of animal shelters in the park's 11 counties. As in any predominantly rural setting, these shelters are overfilled and struggling to save abandoned cats and dogs, to educate on proper care of pets, to teach the importance of spay and neuter programs. Often these shelters have to rely on the kindness of the strangers who visit the Adirondacks for their outdoor experiences.

This book is meant as a fund-raiser for these shelters. Enjoy the hikes, enjoy the park and stop in at a local shelter if time allows.

May you all enjoy happy trails with wagging tails and many happy returns.

Rules and Courtesies for the Trail:

Keep your dog calm around children, other pets and wildlife.

Take proper care of your dog to prevent injuries—beware particularly of rocks, dropoffs, ice and fire towers.

Clean up after your dog, preferably by burying waste four inches deep and 150 feet from any water source.

Keep both you and your dog only on trails around fragile vegetation (particularly above 4,000 feet) and nesting areas.

Be aware of seasonal occurrences such as deer hunting and icy trails and take appropriate precautions.

Veterinary Tips:

What to do if your dog sustains an injury on the trail? Eats toxic mushrooms? Attacks a porcupine or rattlesnake? Or, more likely, what if he simply overheats? Equally likely, what if he runs through poison ivy or oak and spreads it on you?

Westport's Al Haberle, DVM, recommends the following items to put into a day pack for your dog. And speaking of packs, he suggests dogs not carry their own. If off-trail they could get hung up on branches or jagged rocks. Of course, if rules are obeyed dogs won't be off-trail. They'll be well-trained and obedient or, on many trails, leashed. And that's the solution for the poison ivy or oak. A leashed dog won't be able to run through it.

Here is Dr. Haberle's list, followed by his reasons for those recommendations:

- **dog's papers** (even if the dog is chipped)
- **whistle**
- **duct tape**
- **medical supplies:**
    eye ointment (without cortisone)
    buffered aspirin (never Tylenol or ibuprofen)
    bag balm or Vaseline
    Benadryl (Your dog might need a nap after this.)
- **pliers, Leatherman**
- **cap, gloves**
- **small container for water** (but keep an eye out for beavers and be prepared to ask your vet for giardia antibiotics in a couple of days)
- **dog biscuits**

Having your dog's registration and inoculation report in a waterproof container tucked into a pocket probably isn't necessary, but if it is you'll be glad to have it.

A whistle can be heard over some distance, both to summon a dog or to call for help. What's more, it can't be mistaken for a birdcall.

Duct tape can be used for, as we all know, anything. In the case of a dog, let's start with a temporary bootie for an abraded pad (please don't put the sticky side on the dog!). It can hold a splint in place. It can secure a glove to absorb blood from a gash. It can repair a collar.

The medical supplies are pretty self-explanatory as they are generally part of a first-aid kit. For aspirin in case of pain, a good rule of thumb is to give less than a human dose. You know your size and your dog's weight, so take it from there. Same with Benadryl, in case of an allergic reaction to something like bee stings. It's probably never going to be required, but like those papers, if you need it you'll be glad to have it.

Pliers might be able to remove porcupine quills, but if there are more than a couple, or if they're in sensitive places (like the face or mouth, where they're most likely to be), it's better to go to the nearest vet. Under no circumstances should you break or clip the quills! In case of rattlesnake bite, a snake that holds on to the dog is injecting venom. There's time to get to a vet without running, but go immediately. And don't harm the snake, it's dangerously illegal.

The cap and gloves can be cut up if need be for bandages.

A drinking bowl serves as reminder to keep your dog hydrated and you won't have to worry about overheating. If signs of stress appear, stop walking and find a cool spot to let your dog recover. Take care not to offer too much water at one time.

Dog biscuits aren't just tasty treats; they're not even just for dogs. Today's biscuits can be consumed by dogs and humans for extra strength in case you need to exert yourself over your dog's behavior. (Better for you to eat the biscuits than for the dog to eat your gorp.)

If your dog sustains an injury that requires being carried out, Dr. Haberle suggests that, if possible, you own a miniature poodle. If that doesn't work, remember that the Department of Environmental Conservation (DEC) might be able to help.

And that's another reason to sign in at the trailheads.

Introducing the Young Dog to a Trail

One way to have a trailwise dog is to start early, helping your pup learn to follow good examples in the wilds. We've had three litters of golden retrievers, and before they went to their real homes we made sure they had some fun moments in the woods and waters.

Introducing a retriever to water is not always as natural as you might think. When our pups were six weeks old we took them to a small, secluded beach where they could wade cautiously while their parents swam after sticks. The instinct to follow Mom was strong, but we kept them from dog paddling, confining them to the shallows. When they were unafraid of little waves we shepherded them into deeper water, ready to turn them back when they lost confidence in their footing. On shore, we toweled them off quickly; wet puppy fur has no insulating value and could cause a chill.

Teaching a pup about hiking takes the same kind of go-slow approach. Short legs and baby muscles are not up to treks of more than 15 or 20 minutes. Very young dogs are easily distracted too, so a butterfly or bumblebee can lure them out of reach. Before you plan any outing with your youngster be sure he or she will come when called—or at least not run the other way. A little basic obedience work in the yard pays off well on the trail.

—Elizabeth Folwell

Reflecting over Upper Siamese Pond.

Photograph by Bill Ingersoll

Sawyer Mountain

Distance: 2.2 miles round trip **Elevation:** 2,610 feet (800-foot ascent)
Difficulty: Moderate

When my husband and I had three 10-week-old pups waiting to be picked up by their new owners, we took our family of five four-leggers for an introductory hike. The trio had plenty of energy, were as athletic and coordinated as could be expected, and still paid close attention to what their parents did. So, on a still, dry summer day with temperatures in the 70s—ideal hiking weather—we headed up Sawyer Mountain, a hillock near Blue Mountain Lake.

This out-and-back trail doesn't get much use, and when we pulled into the parking area we knew nobody else was on the mountain. Excellent. Running into other dogs or kids on this first outing would have complicated matters. We carried the pups a bit up the trail so they were aimed in the right direction, then let their parents go ahead.

For the first quarter-mile, where the trail has gradual ups and downs and some pup-size stream crossings, our little troopers ricocheted on and off the shady path, never too far from the adult humans and canines. The kids explored roots and mossy rocks, pawed at rotten stumps, sniffed ferns and tumbled and tussled with each other. As the trail began to climb they fell into line behind the big dogs. They kept walking, nearly to a slanted rock where a sliver of the High Peaks is visible. Here we had to ferry them over a steep spot, then all took a 10-minute breather. Magnolia and Burr, the parents, stretched out in the damp undergrowth, and soon their brood was dozing. Let sleeping dogs ...

Our hike had no schedule, something to keep in mind when taking a young dog into the woods. Peak-bagging with a puppy is no fun for anyone, and potential problems abound, from exhaustion and dehydration for the pup to lost tempers for the owner. If your animal is clearly flagging, rest, turn around and try again another day. Avoid hot days and exposed rock. Dogs sweat not just by panting but through their paws, and a rock surface that feels warm to you could be a steam bath for your canine companion.

One cool dog on Ampersand Mountain.

Restored by a rest and snacks (biscuits for the big dogs, soggy puppy chow for the kids, water for everyone) we headed for the top, a rounded knob with an orchard of stunted cherry trees. From there we could see Blue Mountain Lake, oddly slanted as if it would all pour out. This trick was caused by a ridge intersecting the view. To the south we could see Wakely Pond and bright green wetlands. Once again everyone took a catnap. We piled pups in our laps and congratulated the adults on being good and gracious leaders. We checked the little ones for sticks stuck in their fur, sore paw pads and bug bites.

The trip down started as a mad scramble. Then they slowed to a deliberate but steady walk. We stopped at the halfway mark for another rest in the shade (this route is almost never in full sun) and more water and snacks, though not enough food to upset stomachs. Bloating from too much food and water happens easily after a dog has been exercising.

As we approached the parking area we scooped up the trio of pups, who were by then caked with mud and dog-tired. Burr and Magnolia would have gone up the trail again, but moments after they were settled in the car they were snoring along with their kids. When we got home all were awakened by the familiar crunch of gravel beneath the tires. We cleaned up the pups, checked again for trail debris (even in their mouths) and settled in for the evening. The big and little dogs stretched out on the deck like tawny fur rugs, with twitching feet and muffled yips and barks as they dreamt of their day on the mountain.

DIRECTIONS: The trailhead is on the west side of Routes 28/30 between Indian and Blue Mountain Lakes, 4.5 miles west of Indian Lake.

—Elizabeth Folwell

Paul Smiths Visitor Interpretive Center Trails

Distance: Covers 14 miles   **Difficulty:** Easy

Take your dog for a heart-pumping run, or simply stroll along the trails and smell every wildflower. The Adirondack Park Agency Visitor Interpretive Center (VIC) at Paul Smiths, maintained by New York State, offers a variety of dog-friendly trails that will keep both canine and canine walker coming back for more.

The VIC allows leashed dogs on more than 14 miles of trails during the non-winter months. Winter trails are for humans only.

The VIC trail system is categorized by interpretive and backcountry trails. The six miles of interpretive trails are bark-surfaced and offer leaflets and signage guides to surrounding flora and fauna. The eight miles of backcountry trails convey a wilder experience, where the paths' surface is similar to those in the state Forest Preserve.

Interpretive leaflets and trail maps are available at the VIC's front desk for the 0.8-mile Heron Marsh trail, 1.2-mile Forest Ecology trail and 1.3-mile Boreal Life trail. Signs are found on the 0.7-mile Shingle Mill Falls trail, 0.8-mile Barnum Brook trail and 0.9-mile Silviculture trail. These routes are easy on the knees and are good for a quick stroll or combining into a longer trek.

For the backcountry trails, walkers should be prepared for a wilderness experience, including mud, rocks and possible blowdown. These routes can be reached from the VIC building or from a trailhead on the nearby Keese Mill Road. The 2.3-mile Black Pond loop is accessed directly from the Keese Mill Road and leads walkers to the Long Pond trail. Both bodies of water offer excellent brook trout fishing, and Black Pond is known for its resident loons in the summer. (If a loon's yodel is an unfamiliar sound for your dog, it's always fun to watch his first response to the quavering notes.) The Woods and Waters Connector trail joins the Black Pond loop with the Silviculture trail, and the Long Pond trail connects to the Jenkins Mountain trail, a 4.1-mile route from the VIC to the summit (one way), where you and your dog can enjoy views of St. Regis Mountain. Maybe your dog will only enjoy your pleasure, but dogs live to make us happy.

Any one of these is filled with scenic beauty: the wild expanse of a busy marshland, the cozy embrace of a balsam thicket, the open arms of a hardwood forest, the

Photograph by Lisa Godfrey

Ready to go on Nun-da-ga-o Ridge.

companionship of a meandering and babbling brook, and floating feeling of walking through a peatland and bog. Bogs, like loons, offer opportunity to see your dog react to something strange. It may take some effort to coax him to trust staying by your side on such unfamiliar terrain.

The VIC's 2,885 acres are filled with many types of habitat, and that makes it a great place to watch wildlife. It is designated as a New York State wildlife viewing destination, which means you must take extra precautions to control your dog. Opportunities to see moose, white-tailed deer and black bear might not occur if your dog is excitable, but common loons, bald eagles, hawks, turtles, great blue herons and smaller birds and mammals are easier to spot, especially if you are attuned to what your dog notices. My suggestion is to visit during the crepuscular times, as this is when wildlife is more active and visible.

If you're like me, you like to rest along a trail and soak in the peace and quiet, maybe wait for an otter to swim by in the Heron Marsh. There are plenty of benches along the interpretive trails for you and your dog to kick back and, perhaps, share a dog biscuit. Plus, there are two lean-tos on the Heron Marsh trail, two on Black Pond and one on Long Pond. All are for day use only; overnight stays on VIC property are prohibited. Water is abundant on most trails, so it is unnecessary to carry extra water for your dog.

DIRECTIONS: Paul Smiths VIC is located at 8023 State Route 30 in Paul Smiths, 1 mile north of Paul Smith's College. The building is open from 9 am to 5 pm Tuesday to Sunday except Thanksgiving and Christmas. The trails are open from dawn until dusk every day. Admission is free. For more information, call (518) 327-3000 or visit the trails page on the VIC Web site, www.adkvic.org.

—Andy Flynn

Silver Lake Mountain

Distance: 0.9 miles one way   **Elevation:** 2,274 feet (900-foot ascent)
Difficulty: Moderate

Silver Lake Mountain is a hike I recommend to folks looking to escape heavily trafficked High Peaks trails. It's a trek that offers a pretty view of this slice of the northern Adirondack Park—Silver Lake and Taylor Pond below, Whiteface in the distance. It's a route I've described again and again as an easy up and down that you can cover before heading to work in the morning. But I should mention that in the half-dozen times I've hiked it, on three occasions I've had to turn around before reaching the summit: Once with a toddler who couldn't make it up the last rocky, steep section; the next with my arthritic Lab mix, Gwen, who refused to even attempt to maneuver her long, stiff doggie legs on the final stretch; another when my husband's temperamental knee picked this route to protest. That said, this is a lovely hike for healthy people, probably over the age of two, and their healthy dogs who want a relatively Adirondack Lite mountain experience. Really, this route was no biggie for a senior friend, her two Weimaraners and me on a drizzly autumn morning. (All four of us brightened the scenery by wearing orange, since it was deer-hunting season.)

Silver Lake Mountain trail's parking area, a quick right if you're driving northwest on Silver Lake Road, between Au Sable Forks and Hawkeye, in Clinton County, is easy to miss. But if you pass it and end up at the Douglas Resort Beach House, you're less than a mile away. Just backtrack—something I've also had to do more than once. After you sign in at the trailhead the route, a well-maintained easy-on-paws path, starts out as a gentle slope through the woods. You'll come to a couple of clearings with not much to see, but which serve as good spots for you and your four-legged companion to hydrate. Then the trail gets steeper. I've seen and heard various critters along the way, which is why it's a good idea to keep your pet on a leash.

The view from Silver Lake Mountain.

As the trail continues to climb you'll swing around a couple of boulders and then it's just that final scramble to the summit that requires four limbs—for dogs, of course, but humans too. After reaching the top you're on a fine, open forehead with all sorts of ledges and those panoramic North Country views.

DIRECTIONS: The trailhead is about 11 miles northwest of Au Sable Forks on Silver Lake Road in Clinton County.

—Annie Stoltie

Poke-O-Moonshine Mountain

Distance: 2.4 miles round trip **Elevation:** 2,180 feet (1,280–foot ascent)
Difficulty: Moderate

A clear winter morning and unseasonably mild temperatures were ideal ingredients for a hike up Poke-O-Moonshine Mountain. A grand edifice when viewed from the Adirondack Northway, Poke-O's massive ice-coated cliffs make it a popular destination for technical climbers. (According to the Adirondack Mountain Club's *Guide to Adirondack Trails: Eastern Region*, the name came from the Algonquin words "Pohqui" and "Moosie," meaning "broken" and "smooth," and was corrupted by early settlers into its current form.)

Fully aware of the fast-changing weather in the Adirondack Mountains, my daughter, Jenny, visiting from Wyoming, and I packed appropriate gear, including snowshoes, Yaktrax and hiking poles, and made sure Atigun, Jenny's zealous year-old black Labrador, could handle traversing hard-packed snow. Atigun, named after a valley in part of Alaska's Brooks Range, has lots of hiking experience; she carries her own pack for longer trips.

We wore light fleece as we hiked to the trailhead at the south end of the campground (closed in 2009 by the DEC) where we picked up an interpretive pamphlet ideal for naturalists pining to learn more about their surroundings. To our delight, we were the first to sign in that afternoon, guaranteed to have the mountain to ourselves—at least for a while.

The hike almost immediately became a steep climb. Approximately half a mile up, a side trail to the right offered great views of a mammoth rock face to the north, where in spring peregrine falcons nest and rock climbers dangle (though climbers' routes are often closed here during nesting season). We decided this was a good spot to have a snack and hydrate, while carefully keeping the bold and curious Atigun away from the steep drops.

Poke-O-Moonshine's trail continues as a steady climb, and the path grew icy until, at 0.8 of a mile, it flattens out at the site of the remains of the fire tower–keeper's cabin. A short diversion to the left brought us to a lean-to with a near-

Photograph by Lisa Godfrey

Dog tired on Mount Jo.

by outhouse. Another detour to the left, not far up the trail from the cabin, offers an incredible view of Whiteface and Giant Mountains. Atigun preferred listening to the *tap, tap, tap* of a nearby woodpecker.

The last portion of the trail was a gentle climb. When gaining elevation the forest is predominantly a mix of birch, aspen, and red and white pine. Soon we arrived at a bald summit crowned by the well-known fire tower. The original structure was built of wood in 1912, but replaced by a steel tower in 1917.

The wind was cool and brisk, reminding us we were smart to consider weather at the summit while at the base—we happily donned jacket, hat and gloves.

On a cloudless day like today we could enjoy spectacular panoramic views of Lake Champlain, with the Green Mountains of Vermont as its backdrop. Turning to look west or south, we noticed the ski trails on Whiteface Mountain and the fire tower on Hurricane Mountain provided landmarks.

The return trip was much quicker with our poles and Yaktrax, and Atigun had no trouble negotiating the precarious path. She did, however, have trouble staying awake on the drive home.

DIRECTIONS: The trailhead is located off Route 9, either 3 miles south of Adirondack Northway Exit 33 or 9.3 miles north of Exit 32.

—Joanne Kennedy

Azure Mountain

Distance: 1 mile **Elevation:** 2,518 feet
Difficulty: Moderate

Every time I climb Azure Mountain, in Franklin County, our goldendoodle Heidi climbs it three times. Run ahead—dash back, "Come on, humans!"—tear off up the trail again, scurry down—"What's taking you so long?"—you get the idea. Descending, she plunges on, appearing only for occasional checks on our progress; we hardly see her until she turns up resting by our car at the trailhead.

Azure is a monadnock in the northern Adirondacks with one of the best views in the entire park (your dog won't care about this, but you will), stretching from Canada to the Great Range. The trail is one mile long, unrelentingly steep for its final four-fifths. A healthy animal will have a blast. In fact, this is one of the few ways we have discovered to tire ours out for a couple of minutes. Older or infirm canines, though, will struggle with the terrain.

You will need to bring water for your canine companion, or get one of those "pooch packs" and make it carry its own. Aside from an extremely intermittent stream at the site of the former fire-observers' cabin, there's nothing along the way. There is a wetland a few yards from the trailhead, but according to all the pups I've ever known or observed, of all ages, it's more for rolling in so as to cool off and, perhaps more important, to annoy their masters, than for drinking.

The summit of Azure is open and rocky on its southwest side, with a considerable precipice. This produces the magnificent views, but it also presents a bit of a danger to dogs who are either not particularly attentive or sure-footed. What with loose pebbles, rough surfaces and all, stay attuned to your pet's whereabouts.

The summit also boasts a restored fire tower (go to www.azuremountain friends.com), staffed by volunteers on weekends and holidays from May to October. If your dog is not well socialized to others, pick a less crowded time. As one of those volunteers, I have counted as many as 10 dogs (not to mention up to 200 people) on the mountain on a given day. A couple of those dogs have even climbed the tower, much to my amazement. (I do not recommend this; they may follow

Beagle treat on Saranac Lake's Baker Mountain.

their keepers out of loyalty, then realize where they are and freeze, and carrying a quivering 150-pound German shepherd down fire-tower stairs is not something you really want to do.) Always be prepared to leash your pet; not everyone, especially young children—and Azure is very popular with families—is at ease around strange dogs.

Azure provides a good and enjoyable workout. Overall, I believe it's one of the best "dog mountains" in the Adirondacks.

DIRECTIONS: Azure Mountain is on the Blue Mountain Road, which heads south off Route 458 about halfway between St. Regis Falls and Santa Clara. (The other end of this mostly unpaved forest byway is Keese Mills Road at Paul Smiths.) About 7 miles from 458, just past a spring with a bathtub on your right (I am not making this up), a DEC sign points the way to the parking area.

—Neal Burdick

Dewey Mountain

Distance: Up to 3 miles round trip **Elevation:** 2,080 feet (400-foot ascent)
Difficulty: Easy to moderate

In winter Dewey Mountain is Saranac Lake's cross-country-ski area, where dogs are allowed only on Wednesdays. But once the snow is gone Dewey's trails provide woodsy walking not far from downtown. Ten miles of interconnected ski and snowshoe paths meander across the mountain's north slope. The trails are mostly wide and grassy, leaving plenty of room for supermutts Foxxy and Milo to charge around like yoked oxen, jaws clamped on a single stick, without cutting close to my knees.

You can traverse across the mountain for an easy walk in mixed woods. Or head uphill on one of a half-dozen gentle grades, gaining tree-filtered views of Ampersand Bay and Lake Flower as you climb. The top, at most an hour's walk from the main trailhead, is forested and broad. You can glimpse Kiwassa Lake off the back. The subtlety of the view is actually a plus if you want to avoid crowds; most people seeking a quick hike close to Saranac Lake opt for Baker Mountain, across town. Also, Dewey doesn't have rare alpine plants or thin soils that can be knocked loose by playful claws.

Stay on marked trails since some of them cross private land. If you stray off you also risk leaving the no-hunting zone. With the exception of spring, when the hillside brims with vernal pools and seasonal streams, there's not much water to keep dogs cool, but there is plenty of shade.

Pick up after your dog out of courtesy to other walkers and those maintaining the trails. I don't carry a plastic bag as I do for in-town walks; in the woods, there's the option of using a handful of leaves to move dog waste off the path or away from waterways, digging a shallow hole with a stick, depositing the stuff and filling the hole.

Few take advantage of Dewey in the off-season. Adirondack Lakes and Trails Outfitters, which operates the ski center for the Town of Harrietstown, was looking into improving trails for mountain biking in coming years, so check to be sure access

Getting boulder on Hurricane Mountain.

has not been limited for that. Until then it's a benign place for the hiking canine.

DIRECTIONS: From the intersection of Main Street and Routes 3 and 86 at the Harrietstown Town Hall, head west on Route 3 for 1.2 miles. Just past Algonquin Apartments, turn left at the sign for Dewey Mountain Recreation Area. Park in the lot and walk between two brown cabins. Take a map from the register; there are so many trails that it's easy to get spun around even though they are well marked. The register is not checked in the nonwinter seasons, so carry a compass and topo map in case you lose your bearings.

—Mary Thill

Split Rock Mountain Wild Forest Area

Distance: Approx. 2 miles each way, determined by trail
Difficulty: Moderate

It may be a mouthful, but your dogs will thank you. And you can always tell them in the future just to ask for "Split Rock." This is, for my money, the best view in the Westport/Essex area. It also has sentimental value for me since it was the first place I got to know Sassafras, my sweet North Country Society for the Prevention of Cruelty to Animals shelter girl. My Samoyed, Sebastian, and I had seen her picture in the paper and decided, since she looked like him, we'd just swing by the shelter on our way up one of his favorite hikes and see if she felt like tagging along. Well, yes! She's been with us ever since.

I usually bring water and a bowl—there's almost always water at a couple of spots about halfway, but none at the top. And you'd be well advised to pick up a map, since there are numerous trails in this wilderness area, and it can be a little confusing. The Wadhams Free Library sells maps for $2, and so does Dogwood Bakery, also in Wadhams (while you're at Dogwood's, you'd be a raving loony not to get some cookies, too). If you don't buy a map of your own, before starting trace your route on the laminated one now posted at the DEC sign-in station. On this tour we'll take the yellow trail, which, somewhat confusingly, is shown on the map in red.

From the DEC sign-in, go east on the gently ascending main trail (orange markers) for a few minutes. At the fork, bear left uphill, following the yellow markers. The orange trail, which goes off down to the right, leads to Snake Den and Barn Rock Harbors. The yellow trail proceeds generally northeast, with pleasant ups, downs and flats. After 15 minutes or so it loops sharply off to the right, up and around a small knob. You can stay on it here and do the loop, or find the shortcut to the left. This is the beginning of the blue trail, which swings down left through the woods to parallel the Lake Shore Road. If you take the shortcut, be sure to get back on the yellow trail in the right direction when they all converge, or you may end up doing the loop in reverse (you'll want the second trail with yellow markers, the first being the end of the loop). Sounds confusing, but it's clear on the map, which is a good reason to pick one up.

After winding through the woods for a bit (in winter you'll see the summit through the bare branches up to your right), you start to ascend more steeply. This is a great cross-country-ski route, but somewhere in here I give up and do the last bit on foot—skis are a hindrance in the brush at the top, anyway. (Snowshoes should be OK all the way.) There's a little pass at the top of the steep part. Perhaps a cute handmade sign saying VIEW with an arrow, remains at the fork with the yellow trail.

The trail itself is fairly well established. It swings right (southeast) along the hillside and into a hollow that divides the summit. Footing for humans can be just a little tricky in here, so take care. But here's the great thing about this overlook—it's actually three overlooks in one!

Strike off to the left before the trail gets too far into the hollow, a minor bushwhack of a few yards, and *voilà*—Lake Champlain in all its glory. Spot the knob of rock that looks out directly across the lake onto the mouth of Otter Creek in Vermont. To the left, Camel's Hump, straight ahead the Bristol Gap, to the right Snake Mountain rising from the Champlain Valley. Down below, Diamond Island (two separate rocks most times of year) with its light. Water and a snack for the dogs would be good about now, and any Dogwood's cookies you might have lying around.

The second overlook is an easy bushwhack south over to another bit of rock. Here you get the view south along the Narrows, with Basin Harbor to the left, Barber Point straight ahead, and Giant and Hurricane Mountains off to the far right. The third overlook is across the hollow, and you get to it by picking up the trail as it heads back (north) up the hollow. It's up the hill to the left on the far side of the hollow (west). Look down over our route on the yellow trail, with Clark Road ahead and Whallonsburg to the right. You're facing Giant, Hurricane, and the Jay range. Can you find the sliver of the Lake Shore Road as it comes downhill on the way out of Westport?

To pick up the trail, head back down (east) into the hollow. Follow the path to the left (north) till the hollow emerges onto the hillside, then proceed to the yellow trail. And if you see that big old grandaddy porcupine up there at the third overlook, tell him Hi from Sebastian.

DIRECTIONS: The DEC trailhead for Split Rock Mountain is just a few miles up the Lake Shore Road toward Essex from the North Country SPCA in Westport. Look for it on the right 1.5 miles past Angier Hill Road (or, if coming south from Essex, on the left about 0.2 mile past Clark Road).

—Colin Wells

Goodnow Mountain

Distance: 3.8 miles round trip   **Elevation:** 2,690 feet (1,050-foot ascent)
Difficulty: Moderate

If you're positively stumped about where to hike with your dog during hunting season, consider this well-known peak just south of the big ones. Goodnow belongs to the State University of New York's College of Environmental Science and Forestry (SUNY-ESF) and is posted against big-game hunting.

The parking lot is large, a clue to this trek's popularity. Yet, on a weekday in summer or non-holiday weekend in the fall, you may have only a few others for company. A newer trail is an improvement over a time-honored route, engineered by ESF students to show ecological wonders and protect trampled, wet areas. There are so many boardwalks and bridges and water bars, in fact, you could use this route as an agility course for your dog. He or she, however, would likely prefer roaming the maple, beech and yellow birch forest, sniffing through ferns, sarsaparilla and shade-loving wildflowers.

The path meanders gradually uphill, traversing to unusual plants and trees marked with numbers (pick up a trail guide at the parking lot to interpret them). After about 0.75 of a mile the climb begins on a broad, well-packed route. It has only a few steep spots, with convenient rocks if you need to sit and catch your breath. But upward you go. At about two miles you reach an odd concrete pad where a cabin once stood. A little farther on is a seeping spring, with loads of water for your dog and various amounts of mud, depending on the season. Slightly past that is a two-stall barn, proving part of your hike follows an old carriage road. Horses are sometimes parked there so their riders can continue more-difficult passages on foot, following a very narrow ridge—not quite a knife edge—where trees below grow just low enough not to interfere with a fine view southwest toward the Fishing Brook Range, and make the slope appear not so daunting. The trail dips downhill for a bit, then makes its last climb through big boulders and tight trees. Then you've arrived, on a rocky, open summit with a fire tower that's kept in tiptop shape by ESF students.

Good times on Goodnow Mountain.

A word to the wise: Many dogs happily climb the open treads of a tower. Fewer descend so readily. Don't cajole your dog into the highest tiers without practicing up and down on a lower section. You simply don't want to carry your pet down all that way. If your dog has acrophobia, leave him or her with a friend on the rocks and take yourself up for a fantastic view of the High Peaks.

On this trail you're likely to encounter other hikers with dogs. Hook up your free-ranging Fido or put him/her in down-stay to let other parties pass. You will want to bring water for both of you on this trip, since only the spring near the summit is reliable for pet thirst.

DIRECTIONS: The Goodnow trailhead is on the south side of Route 28N, 11.6 miles east of Long Lake village and about 5 miles west of the Hudson River at Newcomb (or 1.5 miles west of the Adirondack Park Agency's Visitor Interpretive Center).

—Elizabeth Folwell

Baxter Mountain

Distance: approximately 1 mile to summit   **Elevation:** 2,440 feet
Difficulty: Moderate to steep

I love to watch a happy dog. Baxter Mountain in Keene offers plenty of opportunity for excitement, beginning with the car shuffle required if you want to start at one end of the trail and finish at the other—as opposed to starting from either entrance, going to the top, and returning the way you came. This two-car plan might be a pain for people, but it's a real asset for a canine. If there's anything our two four-legged boys consider as enjoyable as a hike, it's the anticipation during a car ride.

A human non-hiker is quick to point out that Baxter offers two great places to eat, depending on entrance or exit: Noon Mark Diner, in Keene Valley (with its well-known pies), or Baxter Mountain Tavern, atop Spruce Hill, that make the extra driving worthwhile. Indeed, he adds, they justify the entire outing.

The usual entrance, from the upper trailhead, leads so quickly away from the highway, and smells so wonderfully piney, that minutes into the expedition the sound of a car comes as a surprise. But then an enchanted forest of hemlocks, that also makes this a fine hike for children, begins and by the time you've gone up the trail-improved steps a quarter-mile in, traffic is a thing of the past.

While winding through a lot of downed timber, take a glance upward at patchy sky to note plenty of trees remain standing. There are no streams along here, but there are soft, sloggy areas where a large dog can coax enough drinking water into his muddy pawprint.

The path is well marked and smooth. The ascent is not a challenge until after the trail divides below the summit, where signs point to Spruce Hill, the Beede Road trail marked in red, and Baxter Mountain, marked in blue. This is where Baxter grows rocks, and the rocks themselves grow substantially within minutes.

We took our most recent hike in early evening of a startlingly hot April day. Both dogs were too involved in the mountain to care as we moved through layers of warmer or cooler air. A chair-shaped rock alongside the trail offered a fine spot for one of us to sit while our older dog recouped from the heat—and received a biscuit as reward for his patience—and his younger companion stretched those long legs

Love on the rocks on Baxter Mountain.

that allowed him to follow me.

From this point it helps to have either a large animal with long legs, one with leaping ability, or one that's small enough to be lifted over some of the higher steps. A two-legged hiker can cheat and use hands on either stone or nearby trees, but the dog is on his own. Here an east-facing clearing offers fine views of the folding hills toward Elizabethtown. Once the summit is reached, there's plenty of room for pets or children to scramble over rocks while those less young at heart settle for a snack and a spreading view of Keene Valley to the south. Beware scrambling too close to the edge, but there are plenty of available safely-located boulders.

To continue to Keene Valley, and that Noon Mark pie, follow the red trail markers toward Beede Road. This downhill is mostly gentle, but on that hot April day the trail was hard to find under last year's leaves, and the soggy spots along the little brook offering the dogs more than a pawprint of water were enough to bog down a fairly hefty hiker. This part always seems a little longer than it is, yet the clearing indicating the end of the hike nonetheless appears abruptly. A sign not far above the trailhead stating you are on private land available for hiking, but not hunting, fishing or camping, serves as warning to leash the dogs before you come to a yard and driveways. It's also a good idea to leash them early in case deer are grazing below, as they were on this wonderfully balmy evening.

Just be sure to save a dog biscuit for those weary guys who get to stay in the car and dream while you enjoy your treats at the Noon Mark Diner or Baxter Mountain Tavern.

DIRECTIONS: The sign for the upper trailhead is on the south side of Route 9N at the top of Spruce Hill, some 200 yards west of Baxter Mountain Tavern and almost directly across the road from a side road. To begin in Keene Valley, turn on Beede Road and follow it until a sign on a tree indicates parking for Baxter on the right-hand turn of a Y. Then walk up the left side of the Y, cross the grass between two houses and find the trailhead on the left.

—Libby Treadwell

Baldface Mountain

Distance: 2.2 miles round-trip hike, plus 2-mile round trip on water
Elevation: 2,230 feet **Difficulty:** Moderate. Requires boat-trained dog

The Baldface trail is lake-access only. Canoeing with your pup across a mile of open water, from Sabael on the western banks of Indian Lake to Baldface Mountain on the eastern shore, can be as scenic and adventuresome as the impending hike.

Public islands, sandy picnic beaches, quiet coves, babbling inlets and outcropping ledges that tempt invigorating jumps into the water await human- and dog-paddlers who take time to play in this fjord-like paradise just south of the trailhead. Indian Lake's unspoiled nooks are as fun to explore by canoe as they are beautiful to observe from Baldface's 2,230-foot summit, which is a mere 1.1-mile scamper from shore.

Once atop Baldface, sweeping westerly views pan north and south along the 12-mile-long lake dramatically backdropped by 3,239-foot Squaw Mountain and 3,899-foot Snowy Mountain, the tallest Adirondack peak south of the High Peaks region. Snowy is crowned by a prominent fire tower. Bushwhackers sometimes veer off-trail below the Baldface summit to behold expansive south central Adirondack vistas from the humbling barren cliffs that give Baldface its name.

Clark's Indian Lake Marina (518-648-5459) on Lakeshore Drive off Route 30 in Sabael rents canoes and motorboats, or you can pay to launch your own boat. Remember to follow boating rules and safety precautions, and beware of wind and weather. Wear a PFD (Personal Flotation Device) and strap an appropriate P(uppy)FD on the pup. In fair weather, allow at least 45 minutes to cross the lake by canoe from Clark's. A white circle painted on a large boulder deep in Normans Cove marks a sandy pullout where you can leave your boat near the trailhead.

The cove, named for a former resident hermit, is pond-size and largely isolated from the main lake by the peninsulas that form its mouth. Find it across the lake from Clark's and slightly north of Indian Lake's northernmost camping islands. The islands and wilds around Normans Cove, and to the south, are open to people and pooches but please keep dogs away from designated campsites. (For camping

Bloomingdale Bog pathfinder.

information visit www.dec.ny.gov/outdoor/24471.html.) Be sure to bury dog waste at least 150 feet from the lake or streams.

Hiking Baldface is generally undemanding, just slightly steep near the top. A half-a-dozen mires will muddy paws, but hiking boots usually find footing on stones and logs. The summit has open play space but use caution if bushwhacking near the cliffs. Bring doggie toys for the beach and treats for the trail; also bring water, a first-aid kit, and an emergency whistle since there is no cell-phone service on the lake or mountain.

And don't worry about your boat once you're hiking; it will probably be fine (some people hide their gear in the woods) and, if not, there's nothing you can do. It's gratifying, when you return, to find everything as you left it and to know that you and your pup and others with whom you've swapped tales on the trail will have tail-wagging memories of one of the Adirondack's most beautiful and varied dog hikes.

DIRECTIONS: To launch at Clark's Indian Lake Marina, turn east from Route 30 in Sabael, in the Town of Indian Lake, onto Lakeshore Drive. The road follows the shore to the marina. The Baldface trailhead is a mile across the lake, marked by a white circle painted on a large boulder in Normans Cove, which is just north of Indian Lake's northernmost camping islands.

—**Tom Henry**

Adirondack Hiking with a Basset Hound

Distance: Sheer guesswork **Elevation:** Not much
Difficulty: Extreme, especially with hard-to-control laughter
Directions: Do not attempt this without a leash.

Hounds are divided into "sight" or "scent" dogs, and basset hounds are all smell: nose to the ground, long ears scooping scents to the snout. Bassets are an elongated nose on truncated legs. They are propelled by their prodigious sniff, second only to bloodhounds. Yet anyone cornered by a pack of baying bassets has no right to the term "fugitive."

If you hike with a basset, you must recognize the trail is nothing . . . and everything. First, the trail is not a path; for the hound it harbors complex molecules left by squirrels or deer. You can't see these, of course, but allowing your basset to lead will result in hours of bushwhacking adventure. Bassets will dive under bushes that cannot accommodate your height, even if you're forced to follow on the dumb end of the leash—with a basset your end is always the dumb end.

Any hike with a basset will not involve the High Peaks. Basset is French for "low," and while that does not mean they prefer low terrain, for them any climb is steep. A basset leg is no more than 10 inches long (while the body stretches more than four feet). Likewise, consider this: books on how to nurture one of these diminutives forbid their climbing even *stairs* for the first year. So when you get to the trailhead, realize you will not reach the summit. No panorama for you. You must simply enjoy the tranquility. Your basset will attempt the trail, ears flopping, pulling you toward choice scents, until the climb turns strenuous. Then your hound will lie down, exhaling with a great vibration of jowls.

Bassets can weigh 70 pounds. They recline like boat anchors, with stubby legs and enormous paws tenaciously resistant to motion. So enjoy the moment. This is Zen hiking. You have to extinguish desire, adopt stillness. If you must continue, a pocketful of dog biscuits is your ally. A basset will rise to the treat every time. This propensity is so recognized that some basset owners refer to themselves as "food slaves." You will not get much higher on the trail without repeated bribes, and eventually you will be forced to descend.

Other necessary gear includes what I call the "Adventure Dog Bag"—a canvas tote equipped with plastic bags for gathering the end product, biscuits, a water jug

What? Me hike?

and an aluminum pie plate. The dog will want the pie plate filled with water, and will drink heartily if you hold the plate—exposing you to the splashing of joyous drool. Endure this as a canine-induced martyrdom. You brought this on yourself. You brought this low-achieving, ungainly and headstrong dog to the Adirondacks. Hiking with a basset is a collaboration between your expectations and the animal's inclinations. After returning home he will look up at you with limpid eyes, thankful the ordeal is over. Nothing quite rivals the gratitude of a basset. That must be reward enough.

—Naton Leslie

First Brother

Distance: 3 miles round trip   **Elevation:** 2,940 feet (1,437-foot ascent)
Difficulty: Moderate

Never mind the High Peaks dog-leash law. This morning I'm hiking with my friend Carol and her sister's seven-year-old dog, Fred. Fred is a beagle—sometimes Carol refers to him simply as "Beagle." If you know anything about hounds, you know that, leash law or not, Fred needs to be tethered. Even though this sweet, floppy-eared, bowlegged critter is one of the best-behaved pups I've ever known, especially on the trail—he's experienced; those stubby legs trekked Colden and Marcy in one day— Fred is slave to his eager beagle genes. Rabbits, deer, coyotes, especially coyotes, send him into a howling, braying fit, and then in persistent pursuit. Waddling Fred never does catch up to the hunted, but he's earnest, tailing whatever it is until the scent grows cold, and that can mean hours hunkered down on a rock or a log, worrying and waiting for Beagle's return.

That said, as soon as we begin hiking, something must have wafted past, because Fred propels into beagle mode—only this time, with a 10-foot bungee cord attached to his harness and clipped to my beltloop. (A properly fitting harness is better on the trail than a choke collar, offering more leash control and comfort.) So we continue along the slightly muddy path. Our plan is to climb First Brother, a peak whose siblings, Second and Third Brothers, increase in elevation and provide a popular route to Big Slide Mountain.

It's a perfect little trek—beyond lichens, moss, shrubs and trees with their early-season, too-yellow green hue, like overexposed film, and past a picturesque stream that we cross by hopping stone to stone and through which Fred splashes. From here the trail is moderate: steep enough that you work your lungs and feel the muscles in your legs. First Brother's bare, rocky summit offers a gorgeous view—nice for snap-happy visitors who aren't ready for a big hike but want a sweet vista. You can see the Great Range and, today, a white-capped Mount Marcy way off to the right, the last peak to lose its snowy cover.

Here Carol and I plop down and chat while Fred, still tethered and kept away from the edge, munches on biscuits and laps water from the lid of a CamelBak. Carol and her sister usually dump water for Fred into the cap of a Nalgene bottle or into a crevice in a summit; like lots of fussy dogs, he turns his nose up at the floppy, portable pet dishes peddled by gear shops. (It's best to know this before reaching a mountaintop with a dehydrated pooch.) Fred tries forging on, like he's ready for two more Brothers and then some, but after realizing we're going nowhere, he finds a comfy spot and shuts his eyes.

Hiking with Fred is a pleasure because he's well trained. Sure, there are moments when the bungee cord is taut, particularly on the steep sections when this little guy, about the size of a large tomcat, is tugging me up. Same goes for our descent, when Carol, to whom Fred's now clipped, has to say, "Beagle, wait." (Never let a dog pull you up or drag you down a mountain—if either of you slipped it could be dangerous.) But he stays ahead of us on the trail, only occasionally veering the opposite way or tangling himself around a tree.

Fred's pace is steady as we walk the last stretch. It's late morning and I'm ready for a nap, but Beagle isn't phased. Even now in the back seat of the car, head hanging out the window, he's waiting to see where Carol is taking him next.

DIRECTIONS: From Keene Valley (Route 73) turn west on Adirondack Street, which is marked by a yellow-on-brown DEC sign and becomes Johns Brook Lane. The Garden parking lot is 1.6 miles from Route 73.

—Annie Stoltie

High Peaks Leash Law

I have a Labrador retriever mix who never leaves my side during hikes (no thanks to my training skills—Gwen is just exceedingly conscientious and needy). That it's illegal for her to join me in the High Peaks without a tether has kept us away from this area, which is probably the point. However, I understand that, like most privileges in life, it takes just a few inconsiderate people to ruin things for the rest of us. I've heard the stories about unruly dogs who tear up, down and off trails, nip hikers and other canines, chase wildlife, and crush the mountain-high buzz of folks trying to enjoy the solace of a spectacular summit. I can't blame the dogs—it's their humans, irresponsible enough to let that happen, who raise my ire.

Carol (see above) thinks a permit system is a solution: dogs who pass a test with their owners should be granted carte blanche in the High Peaks. Of course, it wouldn't apply to Beagle, she adds. **–A.S.**

Little Porter Mountain from the Garden parking lot in Keene Valley

Distance: 3.2 miles round trip   **Elevation:** 2,779 feet

Difficulty: Gentle to Moderate

A forecast promising mild temperatures added to an Adirondack blue sky were enough incentives to entice my friend Tracy and her canine companion Riley to join me in a relaxing fall trek up Little Porter. We chose to take the most direct route to the open summit, so started at the Garden in Keene Valley. (In 2000 and 2001 the Adirondack Mountain Club relocated much of Little Porter's trail to avoid private driveways and houses.)

We arrived at the parking lot at eight in the morning, happy to see several parking spots still available. We paid a parking fee and signed in at the trailhead. A quick glance at the register indicated we would have the wilderness to ourselves, at least for a while.

For the first 0.2 miles we followed the Big Slide via the Brothers trail to a junction where our trail veered right. Soon we approached a new bridge over Slide Brook, where Riley was eager to have a cool drink. While he quenched his thirst, we enjoyed watching the clear water sparkle and splash over moss-covered boulders. From Slide Brook the well-marked trail climbs gently and at a mile passes the site of an old sugar camp. Riley had no problem negotiating the small steep section and switchbacks that followed.

We soon arrived at a sign bearing these words: "Jim Goodwin cut out this trail in 1924 at age fourteen. His contributions to the Adirondacks and its trails have been countless ever since. The rebuilding of this part of this trail in 2000–01 was sponsored in part by his many friends and admirers." Unfortunately, Riley doesn't read, but we thanked Jim Goodwin in his stead.

The uphill continued at a moderate pace with several rock staircases to assist our climb. A gray squirrel briefly caught Riley's attention but he paused only for a moment. Soon we reached a junction at the top of a ridge at 1.8 miles. Another 30 yards to the right, and we arrived at the rocky summit of Little Porter. Even with the trees just beginning to turn color, the views were incredible. Tracy shared some

Little Porter Mountain's irrigation system.   Photograph by Joanne Kennedy

of her water with Riley before he stretched out on the sun-drenched rocks to enjoy a well-deserved rest.

We lingered for a while, referring to our map to identify the many High Peaks that lay before us. All too soon Riley was eager to lead the way on our descent. Little Porter was definitely going on our Yearly Hikes List—such a great reward for such little effort.

(For those wanting a longer hike, the trail continues another two miles to the summit of Porter Mountain.)

DIRECTIONS: From Keene Valley (Route 73) turn west on Adirondack Street, which is marked by a yellow-on-brown DEC sign and becomes Johns Brook Lane. The Garden parking lot is 1.6 miles from Route 73.

—Joanne Kennedy

Crane Pond from Route 74
Distance: 6.2-mile round trip   **Elevation:** 1,081 feet (200-foot gain)
Difficulty: Easy

Crane Pond, a beautiful motorless lake, was in the headlines in the 1990s over vehicular access. It's easy to understand why people would want to keep driving the gravel road from the east side of Schroon Lake to this lovely picnic and camping spot. Crane Pond Road, despite the DEC's attempts to close it, remains open. This trail, to the same spot, gets little use, making it a perfect route for man and beast.

The parking area, marked with brown-and-yellow signs for Crane Pond Road, barely holds four cars, but it's rarely full. The trail is almost invisible once you head out, just a narrow path between bushes (raspberry bushes, so watch for prickers and don't eat all the berries on your way in). The path continues as a slim track for nearly half a mile, with a few easy stream crossings and a couple of plank bridges. From one of these you can see, at eye level, an amazing beaver dam holding back a huge flow, with resident ospreys. If your dog is tempted to go for the muck, beware: this is one big wetland with lots of goopy shoreline, plus hundreds of frogs. Swamp ghost trees hold stick stacks of heron nests, like Dr. Seuss drawings.

After the flow, the mixed forest gives way to enormous, beautiful hemlocks with little understory, perfect for that dog who loves to wander and still stay in contact with his human pack. The trail here, for more than a mile, seems to be an old road, quite level. About halfway to the pond some nice rock outcrops appear beneath the trees, shining in filtered light.

The trail moderates from ordinary footpath to old wagon road until you reach the gravel of the road to Crane Pond. Follow this for about a quarter-mile to another parking area, where there are huge pines and hemlocks, virtually no leafy vegetation and occasional refuse left by thoughtless campers. Head straight for a cluster of big rocks in the sun on the shore, and let Buster dog paddle and take in the view. A curious loon may float nearby or an osprey circle overhead. If you want a suitable place to swim, follow the roadway another quarter-mile to sloping rocks in a deeper section of water.

Playtime at Crane Pond.

This is a trip with lots of water for your pet to enjoy and drink, yet a dry trail to walk. In winter, if there's plenty of snow, it's a fine ski trip. However, the thick forest does not let as much snow down as in more-open places, so be sure there's at least 18 inches on the ground elsewhere in the eastern Adirondacks.

DIRECTIONS: The trailhead is between Severance and Paradox, on the south side of Route 74. Drive 4.2 miles from the junction of Routes 9 and 74 (Northway Exit 28), north of Schroon Lake village.

—Elizabeth Folwell

Deer Leap

Distance: 3.4 miles round trip   **Elevation:** 1,100 feet
Difficulty: Moderate

Lake George views lure hikers, year round, to the Tongue Mountain Range in the southeastern Adirondack's Lake George Wild Forest. Named for its three-mile-long peninsula, the 2,258-foot-high range extends from the west shore, south, to separate Northwest Bay from Lake George's Narrows. Many miles of trails traverse the Tongue whose five summits provide spectacular lake views but require dog-tiring treks over rugged terrain. But one of the range's trails, north of the peninsula, makes a nearly perfect dog hike and offers wonderful easterly views across Lake George from an 1,100-foot-high promontory known as Deer Leap.

The 3.4-mile round trip begins at 1,065 feet elevation at a well-marked Route 9N trailhead located seven miles south of Hague village and about 9.5 miles north of the intersection of Route 9N and the turnoff to I-87's Exit 24 interchange in Bolton. Park in the pull-off and follow a tote road a few hundred feet to the sign-in station on the left. The trail is clearly marked.

Initially, the path is quite eroded as it climbs moderately through a hardwood forest. A small pond on the left is a good place to listen to birds and track wildlife. At 0.6 mile the Deer Leap trail branches left from the main path, which continues more than 10 miles south along Tongue Mountain's ridge to the point of the tongue. The intersection is marked by a milepost. The remaining 1.1-mile spur east to Deer Leap undulates over moderate terrain and offers much improved footing.

The ups and downs of this trail net little elevation gain, and provide only moderate aerobic challenge, but if you and your pup are into jogging, middle portions of the path are well suited. Outcroppings give filtered hints of the lofty vista ahead. At trail's end, stepped ledges offer leisurely picnicking with dreamy cross-lake views to the lakeside village of Huletts Landing. Sugarloaf Mountain rises beyond the east shore. Black Mountain, to the south, soars 2,646 feet and has a fire tower.

Waterlogged water dog at the Ausable River.

Below, motorboats streak the busy blue waters of Lake George much like airplanes streak the sky. Sailboats on the historic waterway appear as toys. In 1758, British Major General James Abercrombie's flotilla of flat artillery rafts, armed radeau (enclosed gunboats), 135 whale boats and 900 bateaux carried thousands of troops north over these waters to Fort Ticonderoga in an unsuccessful attempt to take the fort, then known as Carillon, from the French. The armada, which remains Lake George's most bizarre spectacle, stretched six miles as it emerged here from the Narrows just south.

Whether you're imagining history or out for a nature walk, Deer Leap is a popular trail, so it's wise to keep your dog leashed. Bring water, a first-aid kit, and don't count on cell-phone service. Rattlesnakes live on Tongue Mountain, and though they are rarely seen, it's important to take precautions, especially in warm sunny areas and around ledges and rocks. And bring a camera—views here are timeless and worth preserving.

DIRECTIONS: A sign marks the trailhead on the east side of Route 9N 7 miles south of Hague village and about 9.5 miles north of the intersection of Route 9N and the turnoff to I-87's Exit 24 interchange in Bolton.

—**Tom Henry**

The Pinnacle

Distance: 1 mile each way, give or take a few yards
Difficulty: Easy

This short but lovely hike is one of Westport's best-kept secrets—if I had a dog biscuit for every time someone's told me about how they got lost trying to find it, my dogs Sebastian and Sassafras would be set for life. But it's actually quite easy once you know the route. The gentle mile or so climb is perfect for smaller children as well as pets. Round trip takes about an hour at a moderate pace, including time for the spectacular view up Lake Champlain that takes in Northwest (Westport) Bay, the Narrows and Vermont.

There's water at the beginning and end, where we cross Stacy Brook, and a standing pool or two along the way that only dry up in the dryest of dry spells, so I don't worry too much about water for the dogs. One caution: this hike cuts through private land that's leased to hunting clubs, so it's best not to go during hunting season. Otherwise, the public is welcome.

From the center of town, turn west from Route 9N/22 onto Stevenson Road, which runs uphill past the gorgeous lawn of the Westport Library. Go about a half-mile on Stevenson, past the golf course and over the railroad tracks. Just after you cross the tracks, turn right on Mountain Spring Road, a well-maintained dirt road that heads up into the hills that supply the village's famous water. Go about two miles up this old logging road. It's a great road for non-vehicular activities from horseback riding to biking, so if you're feeling particularly spry you can park at the bottom and walk up from here.

Stay on Mountain Spring Road as you pass McMahon Road on the right, bearing left onto Fish and Game Way where Mountain Spring heads right steeply uphill, over the hump to Mineville (another great walk, by the way). Park at the Fish and Game Club, which is fine even if you're not a member.

From the parking area, go due south along the Doheny trail, crossing the footbridge over Stacy Brook and proceeding past the shooting range on your right. In a minute you'll see the Stacy Brook trail come up from the left, where it tees onto

Top dog on Porter Mountain.

the Doheny trail. Stay on the Doheny trail past the amazing wreck of the blue car, an old '50s-style jalopy that always looks to me like a tree fell on it while a young couple was making out deep in the woods.

A few minutes later you'll come to a large clearing, which is where the logging trucks turned around when they last logged in here a few years back. (Don't ask what this part of the trail looked like before that—it's a little heartbreaking.) The Doheny trail continues on south, but to find the Pinnacle you need to turn right, or north, at this clearing and proceed up the gentle grade. This is the first turn in what will ultimately be a big circle, taking us over the Pinnacle and back down to the Fish and Game Club.

As you near the top of the rise, look out for the ruins of several old stone walls, which are quite easily visible running through the woods. They serve as reminder that parts of these hills were once cleared and farmed.

At the top, you'll come out heading north onto a short stretch of level trail with what looks like a large beaver pond on your left. It's actually a man-made pond with a concrete dam, as I discovered while exploring it a few years back. At the far end of the pond, just before the main trail begins descending again, there's a fork that takes a sharp hairpin right uphill. This is the turn that people miss, I think. The Pinnacle overlook is only a few hundred yards up this little trail.

As you emerge onto the overlook, admire the ruins of the old cabin, with stone fireplace and chimney still intact, but be watchful of your dogs since there are sharp metal edges in the debris of odd bits and pieces scattered around the foundation.

This view is a lesser-known southern counterpart to the more popular view from Coon Mountain in Wadhams. Where Coon looks south onto Westport, here we look north. Coon Mountain is straight ahead, partly hidden behind a large pine tree. Going clockwise, you can see the top of Split Rock Mountain poking up, the great expanse of Northwest Bay, the Westport Country Club building and golf course, the North Shore and the Narrows, and in Vermont Basin Harbor, Button Island, Camel's Hump and Mud Island.

On the return, you can either go left back past the pond and come back the way you came, or turn right at the pond and continue north to complete the circle. The trail becomes a rough logging track, and you'll keep to the right and proceed downhill. Be ready to ford Stacy Brook as you near the Fish and Game Club. Most of the year it's usually low enough for you to cross with hiking boots, rock-hopping style, while your dogs wade and slurp their way through. In spring, however, it can come up to just over ankle height, and you might find yourself bushwhacking right, to come out at the footbridge you crossed earlier.

After crossing the brook, turn right and go around the old reservoir to come out at the parking lot.

DIRECTIONS: Take Stevenson Road uphill from the Inn on the Library Lawn, in Westport, cross the tracks and veer right up Mountain Spring Road. Do not turn. Park at Fish and Game Club.

—Colin Wells

Forever wild.

Stone Valley

Distance: 7.5 mile loop, variable trails
Elevation: 850 feet upstream, 560 feet downstream **Difficulty:** Easy

For a river-oriented outing, Stone Valley between Colton and Hannawa Falls is unsurpassed. Trails parallel both sides of the Raquette River on lands owned by Reliant Energy, St. Lawrence County and the Town of Colton; thanks to highway bridges at either end, a 7.5-mile loop is possible, downriver on one side of the Raquette and up on the other. Or, you can do an out-and-back hike of whatever length you wish.

The site is outside the Blue Line, but it involves one of the major Adirondack rivers, which provides dramatic scenery as it tumbles out of the uplands and into the St. Lawrence Valley. This is the geologic boundary of the Adirondacks, political boundaries notwithstanding.

But your dog doesn't care about any of this. Your dog just wants to go for a romp in the woods, and this is an ideal place to do that. The trails are distinct and well marked, but watch for enticing side paths that lead out of the parcel on the east side.

Water is no problem; throughout the trek the Raquette River is at your feet. Easy access for lapping, playing or flopping is frequent.

A note of caution, though—you are within a hydroelectric project, one of many on this waterway. Prominent signs warn of rapidly rising water thanks to dam releases at the upstream end. These are done for the benefit of both the power company and kayakers. It's easy to find out when kayakers' releases are scheduled, but other releases can be done at the whim of the company. They are infrequent, and you won't be caught in a biblical flood, but do keep alert if you enter the riverbed. If you hear what sounds like a train bearing down from upriver, get back on the trail.

The southern, or upstream, ends of both trails are the more spectacular, with falls and gorges sporting geologic features such as immense potholes. Sometimes the trails approach the rims of these gorges. Watch your pet here; pine needles,

Copperas Pond dog on a log.

Photograph by Julie Robinson

leaves and uneven ground are hazards. (Keep in mind, though, that your dog is probably a lot more sure-footed than you are.)

There is much human history here too. Near the southern trailhead of the "West Bank" trail are the stone foundations of an immense 19th-century tannery, something that will rev up your dog's sniffer to this day. If Fido paws at a small mound of reddish-brown furlike material that looks like buffalo hair, that's exactly what it is, still intact after 125 years; the trail goes through the tannery's dump. Between here and the trailhead is a steel-grate pedestrian bridge over the penstock, which your dog may need some help negotiating. Once past that, though, he or she will be in a dream.

DIRECTIONS: There are four access points to the Stone Valley trails, two on either side of the Brown's Bridge Road bridge over the Raquette River (turn east off Route 56 between Hannawa Falls and Colton; the east-side trailhead requires a right turn onto Lenney Road just after the bridge), and two on either side of the bridge in the village of Colton (for the east-side trailhead, follow signs to the fire station and continue a short distance past it). The two in Colton, at the upstream end of the tract, are the more popular.

—Neal Burdick

Copperas and Owen Ponds

Distance: Southerly approach–0.6 miles to Owen Pond; 1.3 miles to Copperas
Northerly approach–0.5 miles to Copperas   **Difficulty:** Easy

Spring is always embraced with open arms after a typical Adirondack winter and is a great time to stretch out those legs in preparation for a new hiking season. My friend Gretchen dressed Wiley, her seven-year-old German shepherd mix, in a blaze orange vest so she would not be mistaken for her namesake coyote cartoon character she so resembles; we packed snacks and water, and off we went to explore the trail to Copperas and Owen Ponds. This is an ideal family outing with a canine companion, as it is short, fairly level and a great swimming hole waits as your final destination.

We chose the longer, southerly approach, following blue trail markers along the bank of Owen Pond Brook. We took our time, poking along the stream looking for aquatic life. Wiley didn't miss this chance to get her feet wet while quenching her thirst in the clear, flowing water.

An enormous rock, capped with large sprawling roots and a tree lured Wiley to the top. She looked down at us as if to say, "What are you waiting for?" We snapped a few photos of her and continued our journey.

Wiley charged ahead of us checking out the trail, returning quickly to make sure we were following her. Damp spider webs woven across the trail indicated we were the first on the trail that day.

We easily spotted Owen Pond, as the forest had only begun to bud. Wiley again stopped for a cool drink, lingering a while in this pristine mountain pond. Gretchen and I had a drink and a snack while a red squirrel chattered loudly, as though he reprimanded us for trespassing on his territory.

Up ahead, Wiley had no problem navigating the boardwalk built over a wet part of the trail. We admired a trillium blooming to our right, another beautiful sign of spring in the northern forest. This well-worn trail continues as a mix of level and gentle uphill, winding its way through a forest fragrant with birch, balsam, pine and hemlock.

Pack behavior on the trail.   Photograph by Libby Treadwell

Forty minutes into our hike we reached the old lean-to, with a great view of Whiteface Mountain. Following the shoreline of Copperas, and another boardwalk, we found a sign marking the trail to Winch Pond—a hike for another day.

The Copperas lean-to, a favorite site for an overnight, is an ideal spot to hang out. We signed the journal while Wiley balanced on a log that stretched into the pond. The shore of Copperas is lined with impressively large rocks that provide a great resting area after a cool swim. We took a last look behind us before departing to make sure we left only footprints, keeping this pearl of the Adirondacks no different than we had found it.

Copperas in the winter is an easy snowshoe, but cross-country skiing requires at least a foot of snow to cover rocks and exposed roots.

DIRECTIONS: There are two approaches to these ponds. The southerly, easier, one is located on Route 86 in Wilmington Notch, five miles from the junction with Route 73 in Lake Placid and 3.9 miles south of the entrance to Whiteface Mountain Ski Center. The other trailhead is a mile north of there.

—Joanne Kennedy

Lost Pond and Walter Biesemeyer Memorial Lean-to

Distance: 4.2 miles round trip
Difficulty: Easy to moderate

Beautiful sunny skies and the realization blackfly season would soon be upon us prompted an early May hike to Lost Pond and the Biesemeyer Memorial Lean-to in Keene. My furry four-legged friend Jude, a nine-year-old golden retriever mix who spent a couple of weeks of her early life in a shelter awaiting adoption, waited patiently as three of us signed in at the trailhead.

The trail begins at the right side of Crow Clearing and crosses a wooden bridge over a small brook. Gradually the path progressed into a hemlock forest. Energetic Jude continued sniffing as she repeatedly darted ahead and then bounded back to us.

Soon we crossed a brook where red trillium bloomed at the side of the trail, then another brook where Jude stopped for a drink before sprinting ahead. Here the trail became crisscrossed with gnarly roots; to our right we observed another cascading brook tumbling over moss-covered rocks. This trip has bountiful sources of water for your dog to enjoy and drink, yet the trail is usually dry and can be hiked with dogs in any season.

The Lost Pond/Hurricane Mountain intersection is a little over a mile from the trailhead. Here a sign indicates it is 1.9 miles to Hurricane's summit, 0.7 mile to Lost Pond and a mile to the Biesemeyer Lean-to. At this intersection is the Gulf Brook lean-to, where we turned left following Adirondack Mountain Club markers toward Lost Pond. The trail then climbs steadily with a few switchbacks and still held some water from spring runoff for Jude to run around in.

Many birch trees suffered from blowdown here. Side trails along this route can confuse dogs and people, so take precaution and a map. Another mile or so from the lean-to, a trail to the right led us to Lost Pond. Jude quickly waded in and eagerly lapped up the water.

Lost Pond is small, and on this early spring day bare birches provided a back-

Sitting a spell in the Walter Biesemeyer Memorial lean-to.

drop to the ring of hemlocks. Birds twittered in the trees and a pair of ducks floated on the pond's smooth surface. While we basked in the warm sun and enjoyed the peaceful solitude, Jude dashed about exploring the pond's banks.

The Hurricane fire tower is visible to the south from the trail between Lost Pond and the Biesemeyer Memorial lean-to. After Jude took one last sip from the brook flowing under the wooden bridge near the lean-to, we trekked to the car.

Snowshoes are recommended for this hike in winter—for people, anyway.

DIRECTIONS: From just south of the center of the hamlet of Keene, proceed east on East Hill Road for 2.3 miles. Bear left onto O'Toole Lane and go 1.2 miles to Crow Clearing.

—Jean Ryan

Hikes for the Older Dog

Brewster Peninsula Nature Trails

Distance: From 100 yards to 3 miles   **Difficulty:** Easy

NOTE: A section of the Jackrabbit Trail that bisects the Ridge and Lakeshore trails makes the Boundary trail (red markers) leading to–or from–Howard Johnson's in Lake Placid. This segment of the Jackrabbit Trail leads from Lake Placid's Saranac Avenue across the peninsula trails and to Whiteface Inn Lane, then on to Saranac Lake.

It happens to the best of us, and it happens to the best of dogs: age creeps up. It probably slides on more slowly in active dogs, but eventually the day comes when they want to climb that mountain and just can't.

Perhaps they don't process information quickly anymore either, but their noses still work and they still find joy in rooting through leaves and under fallen logs. It's a happy dog that sets out on any expedition, and the nature trails winding along Brewster Peninsula, with a trail along Lake Placid's shore (blue markers) offering one selection and a trail along the gentle ridge above (yellow markers) offering another, have everything found on big hikes but the difficulty. Here the old dog can toddle along at his own pace to enjoy what remains of his days, and you can enjoy watching him.

If you are anywhere in the vicinity of Lake Placid, this extension of the Saranac Lake Wild Forest is within easy reach. Since there is, basically, one long path running from the parking area to the lakeshore, with many trails circling around it, a visit can be anywhere from a smooth straight amble or an hour of winding through the woods. (Think of the area as a spine linked by various dendrites.)

The trailhead is easily recognized by a gate with a stop sign. The trail registry is just inside on the right, below a sign welcoming you to the Brewster Peninsula Nature Trails, and another welcoming dogs but requesting the accompanying humans clean up after them. (Bring your own bags and carry them out, there are no trash receptacles.)

The first of six delightfully informative Sheri Amsel–designed signs is nearby. These laminated descriptions of the woodland's ecology and wildlife (sponsored by local businesses or organizations) tell of Trees, Birds, Forest, Maples, Succession, and Bear Food, and serve as a reminder that your dog's nose, no matter how old, knows more about this trail than you ever could. Here is further proof that there is no such thing as being first out on the trail of a morning.

A gentle walk straight up the spine from the gate brings you to a round clearing with a picnic table and trails leading left, to the lake, and right to the ridge. A couple of rustic benches can be found farther along the path, in case your old dog just wants to sit by your knee, his head resting under your hand for a few reassuring moments.

The ridge trail runs near the road at one point, so be alert about keeping a younger dog near you. The lakeshore trail offers many drinking opportunities, but be aware the bank may be too high in some spots; the dam may offer the best lapping spot.

When I first took my Weimaraners to the peninsula in autumn I feared this was to be our older one's last woodland walk. I wanted him to find joy in his moments—and not be pestered or led astray by the younger dog. No worry. There was enough interest along the trail for the younger dog, who rushed ahead to get to all the naso-information first, then ran back to make sure he hadn't missed anything. The older dog hitched himself over exposed roots, back legs moving almost parallel to his front legs, docked tail aquiver with delight. (One of the reasons to own a Weimaraner is that their hard-headedness makes them refuse to do anything that makes you unhappy—as long as you submit to their simple rules: five hours of exercise every day and constant companionship. That same unwillingness to see what doesn't apply to you prevents them from noticing details of their own lives, such as bouts of paralysis caused by a disintegrating backbone.)

In remission over the winter, he proved exercise is the great cure; after trotting along with cross-country skiers, in spring he took to the peninsula trails like a steeplechaser, flying over exposed roots and rocks. (The trails are maintained too well to offer fallen trees.) The half-hour walk of autumn, covering perhaps a half mile, was replaced with an hour of following every trail (if not every scent) and stretching a stroll into a three-mile hike.

But distance is beside the point here. The sense of a trail is everything.

DIRECTIONS: Take Saranac Avenue in Lake Placid and turn sharply uphill between Howard Johnson's and Comfort Inn. The road is Peninsula Way, but it's the only road between these two unmistakable landmarks. Drive to the top of the hill and continue around the "dangerous curve" to the easily seen gate and stop sign on the left. There is room to park along the side, but please don't block the road.

—Libby Treadwell

Belfry Mountain

Distance: 0.8 miles round trip   **Elevation:** 120 feet
Difficulty: Easy

Many older dogs have enough lung power and stamina to take a steep hill if the footing doesn't strain their aching joints or muscles. Often their owners' bodies have reached the same conclusion, or pinnacle, as is the case in point. If you have the urge to go uphill for a spectacular view, one that includes a closeup of a fire tower, but aren't sure you feel strong enough to take a hike, give Mineville's Belfry Mountain in the Hammond Pond Wild Forest a try. There's nothing to it.

The road up Belfry can't really be called a trail. It's a road—unpaved, but in every sense a road kept cleared and plowed for access to the communications towers at the summit. In many ways this is like a forestry track in western mountains, without introduction through narrow glades, but rather an immediate steep pitch with towering evergreens, that soughing sense of wind in the trees that never quite reaches the ground. But it's very much Eastern forest with a smattering of paper birches and a surface of gray and dusty North Country ore tailings and, if you know your peaks and have any sense of Lake Champlain, you couldn't be anywhere but the Adirondacks.

The uphill here levels out after about 0.3 mile, just before a couple of low utility buildings for the communications tower on the right slope. The only way to turn a stroll here into a hike would be to have a good-sized dog on a small-sized leash. But, if a lack of cars in the small parking area across Dalton Hill Road (7C) indicates you have the place to yourself, it's a gentle climb and simple scamper for those with four legs, once the county road has been crossed.

The fire tower is easy to see as you reach the lower structures, where the wide road narrows to resemble a stony driveway. Cell receivers added to the top of the fire tower make this a perfect spot to call your friends if you have questions about which peaks spread before you to the west, or perhaps to e-mail pictures. The tower is reinforced for climbing, but it is not recommended to do this unless someone else babysits canine companions.

A golden moment on Castle Rock in Blue Mountain Lake.

When leaves are not full, the 360-degree view from the rocky promontory that supports the tower includes High Peaks to the west and north, Vermont's Camel's Hump to the northeast, Lake Champlain and Vermont to the east and southeast, and the undulating hills around Moriah and Ticonderoga to the south. All this and more can be studied while dogs, if leashed, stretch out on the high hot rocks to sun or, if unrestrained—depending on age and curiosity—sniff out their surrounding pee-mails.

Further examination of those rocks, by human eyes, reveals four-inch circular 1940s-era USGS markers that prove you are, in fact, on Belfry Mountain.

The High Peaks aficionado can probably name a quick dozen summits. Even a Lake Champlain Valley girl easily picks out Dix, Giant, Whiteface and Hurricane. It doesn't take a clear day to notice, to the east, the peculiar ore tailings mountain left behind from early North Country iron-refining processes, but it might take a clear day to note the conveyor belts used to move slag ever upward.

The village of Mineville and a patchwork of farms are folded neatly below. Compared to this the level farmland of western Vermont appears flatter than the skillet holding the proverbial pancake, before the Green Mountains cover the eastern horizon.

Nope, there's nothing to this hike, and you and your dog will love it.

DIRECTIONS: From Elizabethtown—take Lincoln Pond Road until a Y, where a sign points Mineville 2 miles to the left. Take the right fork and look for the barrier gate and sign for Belfry on the right.

From Port Henry—take the left between a former gas station on the north corner and two-story structure on the south. Follow a sign for Lincoln Pond and Elizabethtown. The mountain is on Dalton Hill Road, which climbs ever upward to the gate and sign, on the left. Park on the right.

—Libby Treadwell

Hiking State Campgrounds

Though we've highlighted mostly hilly hikes, some of the best dog walks on the wild side are near state campgrounds. There's a day-use fee for the facilities, and dogs must be leashed in the campground proper. But once you're several hundred yards up your route, you can unleash the hounds.

In the eastern Adirondacks, Sharp Bridge campground, on Route 9 in North Hudson, offers access to quiet ponds and miles of trails in the Hammond Pond Wild Forest.

Near Forked Lake campground, off the North Point Road, the 5.5-mile one-way trail to Raquette Lake's Tioga Point is through rolling terrain on some old woods roads and narrow paths. If your dog is small-craft worthy, this hike could turn into a canoe trip back to downtown Raquette Lake; arrange to meet your return boat at one of Tioga's pocket beaches. Hand off the car keys, send your friends back on the land route and paddle south to the village.

From Lake Durant campground in Blue Mountain Lake the trails to Cascade or Stephens Ponds are shady, with mixed hardwood forest along the way. Cascade is especially pretty, with a lean-to overlooking the water; you can also reach this spot off Durant Road, in Blue Mountain Lake, on a little-used but well-marked trail through ferny, yellow birch woods.

Also in the central Adirondacks, Rock Lake, off Routes 28 and 30 between Indian and Blue Mountain Lakes, is a lovely spot with a spectacular view of Blue. The hiking trail to the lake is about a half-mile, but to get to a white birch campsite at the lake's outlet, continue another mile and a half on the broad, rolling snowmobile trail. The trailhead parking area is usually empty, but if there are several vehicles you can be fairly sure people are camping and fishing at that outlet.

Continuing south, the walk to the lean-to on the Cedar River, via the Northville–Lake Placid Trail from the Moose River Plains, is another quiet, contemplative trip. There's ample shade, small streams for wallowing and chipmunks to taunt. Several ponds off the Moose River Plains Road are also good spots for dog companions, offering a swim in cool, clean water as the midpoint—and high point—of your hike.

—Elizabeth Folwell

Photograph by Susan Bibeau

Doggie dip in Middle Saranac Lake.

Additional Facts
You and Your Dog Should Remember

Courtesies of the commons must be honored, no matter how remote, when dogs are allowed on all 2.6 million acres of Forest Preserve in the Adirondack Park. Leash your dog when approaching others, while in camp, and when on summits or around fragile plants. Avoid horse trails. Don't let your dog chase wildlife; it's illegal in most counties to run deer—in some places canines can be shot if caught in the act.

In the 1990s there were many complaints in the High Peaks Wilderness Area that some owners were letting dogs run amok, so for the past several years the DEC has enforced special rules there: Pets must be leashed on all marked trails, at campsites and at elevations above 4,000 feet. There's an especially good reason for the latter. Plants that have clung to the mountaintops since the glaciers' retreat are easily dislodged by digging or jumping paws. Hunting dogs can be unleashed when doing their thing, but dogs cannot be left unattended and must always be under the control of their handler. (Pets, leashed or otherwise, are prohibited on Adirondack Mountain Reserve trails, which connect to the High Peaks.)

High Peaks violators face fines of up to $250. A couple of tickets have been issued each year since the new regulation took effect, the DEC reports. A backcountry skier from Keene got smacked with a hundred-dollar fine in 2003 after rangers observed him with his dog off-leash. He pleaded guilty but asked the judge's lenience since, he argued, it's nearly impossible to ski downhill tethered to a dog.

Probably as a result of the High Peaks leash law, there's been a surge of interest in ski-joring, in which a harnessed dog is tied on a long lead to a belt around a skier's waist. "Most people I know just want to get out and be with their dogs," explains Denise Erenstone, who demonstrates the technique at clinics at Mount Van Hoevenberg Cross-Country-Ski Area, near Lake Placid. "They don't want to be expert at it." Even ski-jorers admit to getting tangled on fast descents, but so far rangers seem to be tolerant of brief bursts of four-legged freedom on downhill runs.

Also, while it's required for pets in the High Peaks, it's a good idea to always have proof of a valid and current rabies inoculation for your dog no matter where you go.

—Mary Thill

Special Goodies for those Tired Dogs

Why not buy extra and drop some at the closest animal shelter?

Cedar Run Cafe & Bakery, Keene, makes biscuits shaped like trees or squirrels, bear and moose. Dogs report form doesn't matter and substance is all: they'd rather eat the biscuits than watch them.

Rivermede Farm Market, Keene Valley, sells peanut butter bears, trail mix trout, Parmesan moose and peppermint pine biscuits, wrapped individually, for $2 each. (If you have a small dog, the bag can do double duty for cleanup along a trail.)

Wadhams Market, open Saturdays 10 am–2 pm from June 26 through Labor Day, sells bone-shaped peanut butter–garlic dog biscuits. About 5 inches long, they are sold individually. The garlic is promised to be useful for keeping bugs and vampires away.

If hiking near Azure Mountain or Stone Valley, Canton and Potsdam might be on your way:

Nature's Storehouse, 21 Main Street, Canton, offers whole-grain biscuits made locally by Arvilla Aldous. The biscuits (2–5 inches) are in the shape of a dog bone, sell for 70¢ each, and come highly recommended by dogs and owners. (Open weekends 10 am–5 pm on Saturdays and noon–4 pm on Sundays.)

Potsdam Food Co-op, 24 Elm Street, Potsdam, sells My Doggie Bites in bulk. They're peanut butter–flavored rounds in the shape of a pawprint and are said to be pleasantly addictive, so watch that bulk. (Open weekends 9 am–6 pm Saturdays and noon–4 pm on Sunday.)

Animal Havens and Helpers in the Adirondack Park

Adirondack Friends of the Animals
PO Box 28
Lake Placid, NY 12946

Adirondack Save-A-Stray
4880 Route 9N
Corinth, NY 12822
(518) 654-6220
www.petfinder.com/shelters/NY61.html
Hours: Sun–Mon 11:30 am–4 pm
Tue–through–Sat 11:30 am–6 pm

Cats Limited of Hamilton County
(518) 548-8732
(voucher program for spaying/neutering of cats in Hamilton County)

North Country Society for the Prevention of Cruelty to Animals
23 Lake Shore Road
Westport, NY 12993
(518) 962-8604
www.ncspca.org
Hours: Tue–Fri noon–4 pm
Sat 10 am–5 pm
Sun by appointment
closed Mon

Purrs and Paws Feline Rescue and Adoption Agency
3857 Route 9L
Lake George, NY 12845
(518) 798-0718
www.purrsandpawsrescue.org
(takes cats from Glens Falls Municipal Shelter after 5 days to prevent euthanasia)
Hours: 10 am–2 pm daily

Red Fern Spay & Neuter Mobile Veterinary Clinic
(518) 645-0178
www.redfernvet.com

Tri-Lakes Humane Society
PO Box 1111
Saranac Lake, NY 12983
(518) 891-0017
www.petfinder.com/shelters/trilakeshumanesociety.html
Hours: Tue–Fri 1 pm–5 pm
Sat 11 am–4 pm
closed Sun–Mon